First published 1981
Second impression 1983
by The Hamlyn Publishing Group Limited
London · New York · Sydney · Toronto
Astronaut House, Feltham, Middlesex, England
© Copyright 1981
The Hamlyn Publishing Group Limited

Illustrations by Victor Ambrus

ISBN 0 600 36484 4

Printed in Singapore by Tien Wah Press

My Little Book of Jesus

NORMAN BULL

HAMLYN
London · New York · Sydney · Toronto

Contents

Baby
Jesus

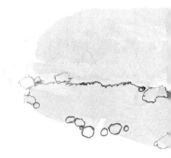

Joseph was very worried as he led his ass, carrying Mary, into the little town of Bethlehem. It was time for Mary's baby to be born so Joseph went to an inn to ask for a bed.

'No room at the inn,' said the innkeeper. 'Go in the stable, if you like.'

Joseph made a bed for Mary in the clean straw, with oxen and asses standing nearby. There,

Mary's baby boy was born and he was called Jesus. Baby Jesus was wrapped up and laid in a manger, safe and cosy and warm.

Soon some shepherds tip-toed into the stable. 'An angel appeared to us,' they whispered. 'He said, "A Saviour has been born. You will find him in a manger at Bethlehem." We have come to worship the new-born Saviour.' Then the shepherds knelt in wonder before Baby Jesus.

Not long after, there came three wise men from faraway in the East. 'A wondrous new star appeared to us,' they said. 'It told us of a child born to be King, and then it led us to Bethlehem. We have come to worship the new-born King.' They laid down precious gifts of gold and frankincense and myrrh. Then the wise men knelt before Baby Jesus.

The boy Jesus

Mary and Joseph lived in a little town called Nazareth. Jesus grew up in their small white house. He helped Mary with her housework and went with her to the well to fetch water. Joseph was a carpenter, making things with wood. Jesus helped him in his workshop so that one day he could be a carpenter too.

When Jesus was five years old, he went to school. He and his friends

learnt to read and write. Then they read their Holy Books, learning about God. When school was over, the boys dashed out to play. They made slings to throw pebbles, and pipes to play music.

When the boys were twelve years old, they left school. Then Jesus and his friends went with their families to the Holy City of Jerusalem. The boys went to talk with the wise men at the Holy Temple, to learn more about God. Jesus loved being with the wise men. They were amazed by his questions and by his understanding of God.

When they began the journey home, Mary thought that Jesus was

with his friends. But that night she
could not find him anywhere. Next
morning, Mary and Joseph hurried

back to Jerusalem. They searched everywhere for Jesus. At last they found him. He was still with the wise men.

'Jesus!' said Mary crossly. 'We've been searching for you everywhere. Didn't you know how worried we must be?'

Jesus was surprised. 'Why did you search for me, Mother? Didn't you know that I must be in my heavenly Father's house?'

Jesus went back home with Mary and Joseph. He was a good boy, and obedient to them. He grew tall, and strong, and wise. He was kind, and thoughtful, and loving. Most of all, Jesus loved God, and he lived close to his heavenly Father.

Jesus the friend of all

Jesus the teacher

'I bring you Good News,' Jesus said to the people. 'The kingdom of God has come on earth. Change your hearts and minds, and follow me.'

Many people followed Jesus, so he needed helpers. Jesus chose twelve men to help him. Three of them were big, strong fishermen. They were Peter and James and John. They were always close to Jesus.

19

God loves each of his children

Jesus told this story to the people.

'There was once a rich farmer with two sons. His money would be shared between them by law. Simon, the elder son, worked hard on the farm. But young Jason hated it. "Father, I want my money now," he said. "I want to leave home and see the world." Jason

went to a big city, where he had an
exciting time with all his money,
but soon it was gone and he was
then a beggar. He found a job
looking after pigs, but he was so
hungry that he wanted to eat pig
food. Jason began to think. "Even
my father's servants don't go
hungry like I do," he said to

himself. "I'll go back home. I'll tell father I'm sorry, and ask him to take me back as a servant."

'His father saw Jason first and ran to welcome him. "Bring the best clothes for my son," he ordered the servants, "and prepare a fine feast." What a happy party it was.

Simon heard the noise as he
came back from work. He was so

angry that he would not join in. "I've always worked hard for you and obeyed you," he shouted at his father. "You never gave me a feast, but what a feast you have for your lazy son who has wasted your money."

"Dear Simon," said his father gently, "you are always with me, and all I have is yours. I had to show how happy I was. My son was lost, and now he is found. You are both my sons, and I love you both dearly. Please, Simon, come and join in the party. Then I shall be full of happiness."'

God is like that father. Our heavenly Father loves each of his children, too.

Jesus shows the love of God

One day, Jesus was talking to the people. Some mothers came with their children, for they wanted Jesus to bless them. The helpers of Jesus were fussy. 'Don't bother Jesus now,' they said. 'You can see how busy he is.'

The mothers turned away sadly. Then the voice of Jesus rang out. 'Let the children come to me. Don't turn them away,' he said angrily. 'They are dear to our heavenly Father.'

Then the mothers turned back and took their children to Jesus, and he blessed them all one by one.

Talking to God

Jesus often left his friends and went away alone, to be with his heavenly Father. One day, his friends said to him, 'Lord, teach us how to talk to God.'

Jesus said to them, 'When you speak to God, say this prayer:

Our Father in heaven,
May your name be honoured.
May your kingdom come.
May your will be done on earth
as it is in heaven.
Give us each day the bread we
    need.
Forgive us what we owe to you,
as we forgive those who owe to
    us.
Keep us from wanting to do
    wrong,
and save us from evil.'

Jesus heals the sick

One day, a blind man was led to
Jesus by his friends. He could just
see the shape of trees, that was all.
'Lord, please lay your hands on
him and heal him,' his friends
pleaded.

31

Jesus took the man away. When they were alone, Jesus put his hands on the man's eyes. 'Can you see anything?' he asked.

'Yes,' said the man excitedly. 'I can see trees walking about. They must be people!'

Then Jesus laid his hands on the man's eyes again.

'Now I can see people clearly,' the man cried joyfully. 'Oh, I can see everything!'

Then Jesus said to him, 'Go back home quietly. Don't go into the town, and don't tell anyone what God has done for you.'

Jesus is betrayed

Jesus was very popular among the people, but the leaders in Jerusalem were worried. 'The people follow Jesus,' they said. 'If we let him go on like this, the Romans will get suspicious. They will fear a revolt against them, and then they will

destroy us and our people.' So the leaders of the people decided, 'We must get rid of Jesus to save our people.'

Jesus knew the dangers that he faced in Jerusalem, but he was ready to suffer and to die, to show men the love of God, and to win them to him.

Jesus went to Jerusalem with his twelve helpers. One of them was Judas Iscariot, who went secretly to the leaders of the people. 'I will betray Jesus to you,' Judas said. 'I know a quiet place where he goes, and I will lead your men to him. They can arrest Jesus there without trouble from the people.'

The leaders of the people were delighted. 'We will pay you thirty pieces of silver,' they promised.

Jesus was in a quiet garden where he often went. Peter and James and John were with him. Jesus was troubled, for he knew what must happen. Then Judas Iscariot came with the men. 'Hail, Master!' he said, giving Jesus the kiss of friendship.

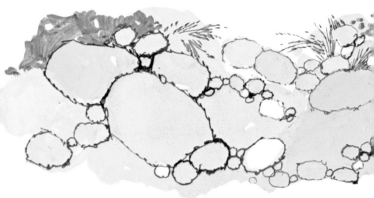

Then the men knew that this was Jesus. They tied his hands together and led him away.

Jesus the Son of God

After his arrest Jesus was tried by the leaders of the people. 'Are you the Saviour sent from God?' they asked.

'I am,' said Jesus.

'He is mocking God!' they cried. 'He must die.' Then they took Jesus to Pilate, the Roman Governor, so that he could order Jesus to be put to death. Pilate soon saw that Jesus was no danger to the Romans, but the leaders of the people wanted to get rid of Jesus, so Pilate gave in.

Jesus was taken to a hill outside
Jerusalem. There, the soldiers
nailed Jesus to a cross of wood, and
made it stand up in the ground.
Jesus said, 'Father, forgive them.
They do not understand what they
are doing.' Jesus hung on the cross
until he died.

Two friends of Jesus laid his body
in a tomb, in a garden nearby. A
big round stone guarded the door
of the tomb. But when friends of
Jesus came back, they found that
the stone had been rolled away.
The tomb was empty, and the body
of Jesus had gone. One woman,

named Mary, stayed there weeping.

'Why are you weeping?' said a voice. 'Who are you looking for?'

Mary thought it was the gardener. 'Oh Sir,' she cried, 'tell me where he has been taken so that I can anoint his body.'

'Mary,' said the stranger softly.

'Master!' she cried with joy, knowing the voice of Jesus.

'Go and tell my friends,' Jesus said.

'I have seen the Lord!' Mary cried when she got back to them.

Jesus later appeared to his friends, but one of them, named Thomas, was not there. 'I will not believe it,' he said, 'until I have seen him myself.'

Soon, Jesus appeared to Thomas, and then he believed too. The friends of Jesus did not see him any more, but they were full of joy, for they knew that Jesus was alive for evermore. They knew that he was with them always.

Still today, those who believe in
Jesus know that he is with them
too, and they worship him as their
Lord and their God.